Let's Recycle

Represent and Solve Addition Problems

Peter Zahn

New York

Published in 2014 by The Rosen Publishing Group, Inc.
29 East 21st Street, New York, NY 10010

Book Design: Mickey Harmon

Photo Credits: Cover Multi-bits/The Image Bank/Getty Images; p. 5 Diego Cervo/Shutterstock.com; p. 7 sunsetman/Shutterstock.com; p. 9 (counter) Venus Angel/Shutterstock.com; pp. 9, 19 (orange can) Fotofermer/Shutterstock.com; pp. 9, 11, 19, 21 (green bottle) anaken2012/Shutterstock.com; pp. 9, 19 (glass bottle) 9comeback/Shutterstock.com; p. 11 (classroom) Glen Jones/Shutterstock.com; pp. 11, 13, 21 (aluminum can) 315 Studio by khunaspix/Shutterstock.com; pp. 11, 21 (box of paper) erashov/Shutterstock.com; p. 13 (aisle) ilker canikligil/Shutterstock.com;p. 13 (tuna can) archetype/Shutterstock.com; p. 13 (box) Blacknote/Shutterstock.com; p. 15 (wall) hkeita/Shutterstock.com; p. 15 (balls) Pavel Hlystov/Shutterstock.com; p. 17 (mailboxes) Media Union/Shutterstock.com; p. 17 (large envelope) Steve Collender/Shutterstock.com; p. 17 (envelope) drfelice/Shutterstock.com; p. 17 (pink envelope) Joe Belanger/Shutterstock.com; p. 19 (park) 1000 words/Shutterstock.com; p. 21 (library) DavidPinoPhotography/Shutterstock.com; p. 22 Morgan Lane Photography/Shutterstock.com.

Library of Congress Cataloging-in-Publication Data

Zahn, Peter, 1986—
Let's recycle : represent and solve addition problems / Peter Zahn.
    p. cm. — (Core math skills. Operations and algebraic thinking)
Includes index.
ISBN 978-1-4777-2109-4 (paperback)
6-pack ISBN 978-1-4777-2110-0
ISBN 978-1-4777-2207-7 (library binding)
1. Addition—Juvenile literature. 2. Mathematics—Juvenile literature. 3. Recycling (Waste, etc.)—Juvenile literature. I. Title.
QA115.Z34 2014
513.2'11—dc23

2013002099

Manufactured in the United States of America

CPSIA Compliance Information: Batch #CS13RC: For further information contact Rosen Publishing, New York, New York at 1-800-237-9932.

Word Count: 284

Contents

All About Recycling   4

Recycling Around Town   8

What's at the Market?   12

More Recycling!   16

Recycling Is Fun!   22

Glossary   23

Index   24

All About Recycling

Do you know what it means to recycle?

When you recycle, you use something again.

Recycling helps the **environment**.

You can recycle things like **plastic**, paper, and cans.

Glass can be recycled, too.

I like to help recycle in my town!

PLASTIC

PAPER

CANS

7

Recycling Around Town

My mom and I recycle things from our house.

We have 10 cans and 1 plastic **bottle**.

We also have 3 glass bottles.

We recycle 14 things from our house.

10 + 1 + 3 = 14

My school has things to recycle, too.

I help my school recycle 5 boxes of paper.

I also find 3 bottles and 2 cans.

I help my school recycle 10 things.

5 + 3 + 2 = 10

What's at the Market?

There are many things to recycle at the market.

I find 4 big cans and 2 little cans.

I find 12 boxes to recycle, too.

That makes 18 things to recycle!

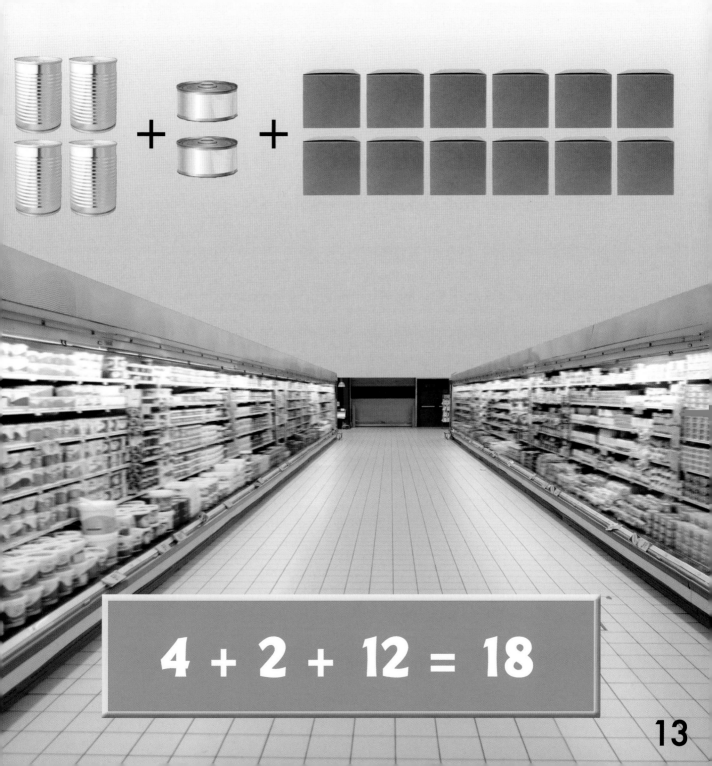

4 + 2 + 12 = 18

Next, I go to the day care in my town.

The day care has plastic toys to recycle.

There are 4 yellow balls and 3 green balls.

There are 5 purple balls, too.

How many toys can the day care recycle?

4 + 3 + 5 = 12

More Recycling!

The post office recycles old **envelopes**.

I help recycle 10 big ones and 9 small ones.

I recycle 1 pink envelope, too!

I recycle 20 envelopes at the post office.

$$10 + 9 + 1 = 20$$

My friends and I help clean up the park.

We find 9 glass bottles and 3 plastic bottles.

We also find 5 cans.

We find 17 things to recycle at the park.

9 + 3 + 5 = 17

The library has a lot of things to recycle, too.

I help recycle 2 boxes of paper.

I also help recycle 4 cans and 1 bottle.

How much can I recycle at the library?

2 + 4 + 1 = 7

Recycling Is Fun!

Recycling is a lot of fun!

It feels good to keep my town clean.

Glossary

bottle (BAH-tuhl) Something used to hold liquids.

envelope (EHN-vuh-lohp) Something used to hold
   a letter.

environment (ihn-VY-ruhn-muhnt) Everything in the world
   that surrounds a living thing.

plastic (PLAS-tihk) A type of matter used to make bottles,
   dishes, and toys.

Index

bottle(s), 8, 10, 18, 20

boxes, 10, 12, 20

cans, 6, 8, 10, 12,
      18, 20

day care, 14

envelope(s), 16

environment, 6

glass, 6, 8, 18

house, 8

library, 20

market, 12

paper, 6, 10, 20

park, 18

plastic, 6, 8, 14, 18

post office, 16

school, 10

Due to the changing nature of Internet links, The Rosen Publishing Group, Inc., has developed an online list of websites related to the subject of this book. This site is updated regularly. Please use this link to access the list: www.powerkidslinks.com/cms/oat/lre